W9-AYR-798

ANIMALS

Hyenas

by Kevin J. Holmes

Consultant:
Jack Grisham
Director/Animal Management
Oklahoma City Zoological Park

Bridgestone Books
an imprint of Capstone Press
Mankato, Minnesota

8501140

Bridgestone Books are published by Capstone Press
818 North Willow Street, Mankato, Minnesota 56001
http://www.capstone-press.com

Copyright © 1999 by Capstone Press. All rights reserved.
No part of this book may be reproduced without written permission from the publisher.
The publisher takes no responsibility for the use of any of the materials
or methods described in this book, nor for the products thereof.
Printed in the United States of America.

Library of Congress Cataloging-in-Publication Data
Holmes, Kevin J.
    Hyenas/by Kevin J. Holmes.
        p. cm.—(Animals)
    Includes bibliographical references and index.
    Summary: Introduces the hyena's physical characteristics, habits, prey, and relationship to humans.
    ISBN 0-7368-0064-6
    1. Hyenas—Juvenile literature. [1. Hyenas.] I. Title. II. Series: Animals (Mankato, Minn.)
QL737.C24H65   1999
599.74′3—dc21

                                                                98-17331
                                                                     CIP
                                                                      AC

Editorial Credits
Matt Doeden, editor; Timothy Halldin, cover designer; Sheri Gosewisch, photo researcher

Photo Credits
Cheryl A. Ertelt, 8
Elizabeth DeLaney, 10
GeoIMAGERY/Bill Webster, 4
Michele Burgess, 6, 16, 18, 20
Susan Kelm/David F. Clobes, cover
Visuals Unlimited/Walt Anderson, 12; Buff Corsi, 14

Table of Contents

Spots

Scruff

Ears

Jaws

Fast Facts

Kinds: There are three main kinds of hyenas. They are spotted hyenas, brown hyenas, and striped hyenas.

Range: Hyenas live mainly in central and southern Africa.

Habitat: Hyenas live in deserts and savannas. Savannas are flat, grassy areas with few trees.

Food: Hyenas hunt animals such as zebras and antelope. They also find and eat dead animals.

Mating: Hyenas can mate throughout the year. Female hyenas usually give birth to two young.

Young: Young hyenas are called cubs. Cubs stay with their mothers for about one year. Cubs spend most of their time in dens.

Hyenas

Hyenas are mammals. Mammals are warm-blooded animals with backbones. The body heat of warm-blooded animals stays about the same. Their body heat does not change with the weather.

There are three main kinds of hyenas. Spotted hyenas are the most common. Brown hyenas and striped hyenas are the other two kinds.

Most hyenas live in large groups called clans. Hyenas in clans hunt and eat together. They also raise their young together.

Hyenas use calls to warn other hyenas of danger. Hyenas also use calls when they hunt for food. The calls tell other hyenas when food is nearby. Some people think hyena calls sound like laughter.

Spotted hyenas are the most common hyenas.

Appearance

Hyenas look something like dogs. They have short back legs and long necks. They have big, round ears that help them hear well. Their large, powerful jaws can crush hard objects such as bones.

Hyenas have long, yellow-brown fur. The fur is darker on their tails and around their noses. Spotted hyenas have dark spots on their fur. These spots may fade as the animals grow old. Striped hyenas have dark stripes on their fur.

Male and female hyenas look alike. Females are usually larger than males. Female hyenas weigh about 120 pounds (54 kilograms). Male hyenas weigh about 100 pounds (45 kilograms).

Hyenas have short back legs and long necks.

Homes

Hyenas live mostly in central Africa's deserts and on savannas. Savannas are flat, grassy areas with few trees. Some hyenas live in southern Africa. In the past, many hyenas lived there. But people have forced most hyenas out of the area.

Each hyena clan has its own territory. Clans mark their territories with scents. Hyena clans usually avoid the scents of other clans. Two clans sometimes fight for one territory. They may do this if there is not enough food.

Hyena clans move around their territories. They follow prey. Prey is an animal hunted by another animal for food. Hyenas' prey includes zebras, antelope, and gazelles.

Hyenas live mostly in central Africa's deserts and on savannas.

Mating

Hyenas can mate throughout the year. Mate means to join together to produce young. Hyenas may mate with many different partners during their lives. Females choose when to mate. They also choose their male partners.

Each clan usually has one dominant female. The dominant female is the most powerful hyena in the clan. The dominant female may mate more often than other females. She usually produces the most young.

Female hyenas give birth about 100 days after they mate. They usually give birth to two cubs. Some females die the first time they give birth. Many cubs die too.

Hyenas can mate throughout the year.

Young

Newborn cubs are black or dark brown. They weigh about three pounds (1.4 kilograms). Their eyes are closed until about two weeks after birth.

Cubs spend most of their time in dens. Female hyenas always stay near the dens. They protect and care for their cubs. Cubs drink milk from their mothers' bodies.

Female hyenas may share dens. Some hyena dens hold up to 20 cubs. All of a clan's cubs may stay in one large den.

Female hyenas care for their cubs for about one year. Most hyenas are fully grown after this time. Some cubs leave their clans after one year. They join other clans. Males are more likely to leave their clans than females.

Cubs spend most of their time in dens.

Food

Hyenas are predators. Predators hunt and eat other animals. Hyenas will eat almost any animal they can catch. They often hunt zebras, antelope, and gazelles.

Hyenas use their sense of smell to scavenge. They search through waste for food. Hyenas often follow lions from a distance. Hyenas eat food that lions do not eat.

Hyenas sometimes follow vultures. Vultures are birds that scavenge for dead animals. Hyenas may eat the dead animals that vultures find.

Hyenas can eat almost any part of an animal. They can even eat bones. Their powerful jaws allow them to crush the bones.

Hyenas and vultures often eat the same kinds of food.

Enemies

Lions are hyenas' greatest enemies. Lions often kill hyenas. Lions do not eat the hyenas they kill.

Lions and hyenas hunt the same kinds of prey. They often steal food from each other. Large groups of hyenas sometimes attack lions. The groups usually kill young or sick lions. Hyenas rarely eat the lions they kill.

Jackals sometimes steal hyenas' food. Jackals are small scavengers that look like dogs. They work in pairs to take a hyena's food. One of the jackals gets a hyena to chase it. Then the other jackal steals the hyena's food.

Hyenas also compete with wild dogs. Hyenas follow wild dogs to steal their food. Groups of wild dogs sometimes fight groups of hyenas for food.

Lions and hyenas often steal food from each other.

Hyenas and People

In Africa, hyenas often live near villages and cities. They scavenge through people's garbage. Hyenas may kill farm animals such as cattle.

Hyenas sometimes attack people. But this does not happen often. Hyenas rarely attack active people. But they may attack people who sleep outside. They may attack very old people or very young children.

It is illegal to kill hyenas in some African countries. Many people kill hyenas anyway. Some of these people kill hyenas to protect cattle. Hunters kill hyenas to stop the hyenas from killing other animals.

Hunters kill hyenas because hyenas kill other animals.

Hands on: Smelling Game

Hyenas use their sense of smell to find prey. How good is your sense of smell? Play this game to find out.

What You Need

Six or more different foods with strong smells
A blindfold
One or more friends

What You Do

1. Let everyone look at all the foods you have selected.
2. Blindfold a friend.
3. Pick a food and hold it under your friend's nose. Ask your friend to guess which food it is.
4. Take turns being blindfolded. See who can guess the most foods correctly.

Words to Know

clan (KLAN)—a large group of animals living together

dominant (DOM-uh-nuhnt)—the most powerful member of a group

mate (MATE)—to join together to produce young

predator (PRED-uh-tur)—an animal that hunts and eats other animals

prey (PRAY)—an animal hunted by another animal for food

savanna (suh-VAN-uh)—flat, grassy areas with few trees

scavenge (SKAV-uhnj)—to search through waste for food

Read More

Rothaus, Don P. *Hyenas.* Plymouth, Minn.: Child's World, 1996.

Silver, Donald M. *African Savanna.* One Small Square. New York: Learning Triangle Press, 1997.

Useful Addresses

**Oklahoma City
Zoological Park**
2101 N.E. 50th
Oklahoma City, OK 73111

Toronto Zoo
361A Old Finch Avenue
Scarborough, Ontario M1B 5K7
Canada

Internet Sites

Hyena
http://www.intertex.net/users/rzu2u/hyena.htm

Predator Exhibit
http://drew.buffalo.k12.ny.us/drew/Tours/Zoo/
PredatorExhibit/PredatorExhibit.html

Index